SECR
STAFFORDSHIRE

GHOSTS, LEGENDS AND STRANGE TALES

Marian Pipe

S.B. Publications

To my Staffordshire friends, Jean, Marjorie and Cyril

Bt the same author:
Tales of Old Northamptonshire
Tales of Old Leicestershire

First published in 1994 by S.B. Publications
C/o 19 Grove Road, Seaford, East Sussex BN25 1TP.

ISBN 1 85770 066 X

Typeset, printed and bound by
Manchester Free Press,
Longford Trading Estate,
Thomas Street, Stretford,
Manchester M32 0JT.

CONTENTS

Front cover: Lud's Church (see Chapter 5)

Back cover: Steps leading down to Lud's Church

Title page: In the middle of the tremendous cliff face of Thor's Crag is the entrance to Thor's Cave. From the massive aperture, which is 20-foot wide and 30-foot high, there are spectacular views over the beautiful Manifold Valley. Tools of the prehistoric man were found on the floor of the cave when it was excavated in 1864 by Mr. Carrington, the school master of Wetton. Artefacts of other periods were also found, such as bronze bracelets and brooches, knives and pieces of Samian pottery.

INTRODUCTION

Staffordshire is an underestimated and undiscovered county for many people. They often make the mistake of thinking the county is a great industrial track of land from the Potteries in the north to the Black Country in the south. In fact four-fifths of the county is rural and contains some of the most beautiful unspoilt and varied scenery in England. From the wild moors and hills of the Staffordshire Moorlands in the north-east, to the postcard west bordering Shropshire, the rich rolling farmland in the middle of the county and the unspoilt beauty of Cannock Chase between Stafford and the sprawling metropolis of West Midlands, the county is full of contrasts and surprises.

Staffordshire also has many legends and strange tales, with towns and villages steeped in local traditions and folklore, and historical tales which are stranger than fiction.

This collection of old tales, many of which have been recorded before, are retold in a colourful and vigorous way which should delight all readers who are interested in Staffordshire's folklore and history.

1. THE MERMAID'S POOL

The Mermaid's Pool, also known as the Blackmere, lies on top of the Morridge Hills, on the edge of the spectacular A53 road between Leek and Buxton, at a height of 1,500 feet above sea level. It is a deep, dark tarn surrounded by peaty soil. Local people of long ago had many superstitions and beliefs about the pool, no cattle would drink from it, no birds would fly over it or settle on its surface. It was the haunt of evil spirits, where devilish deeds were committed. The tarn was also protected by a mermaid. If anyone was brave enough to go near it at night the creature would entice them down into the pool with her, to a watery grave, or if she was in a more kindly mood she would tell them strange tales.

Many generations ago, a ploughman who lived in a village nearby happened to stray close to the pool on night, the mermaid rose to the surface and swam towards him. He was astonished by the sight and riveted to the spot. The creature told him to listen carefully to what she had to say and warned him that if Blackmere should ever burst its banks, the Frith

The Mermaid's Pool, also known as the Blackmere; a deep dark tarn on top of the Morridge Hills, said to be the haunt of a mermaid

and the town of Leek would be flooded and sink beneath the waters.

There is a theory the mermaid originated in medieval times when Joshua Linnet branded a young woman as a witch and had her thrown into the Blackmere. As she floundered in the water she cursed Linnet and said that he would suffer the same fate. Three days later her accuser was found in the pool with his face scratched to pieces, as though with talons.

There seems to be some truth for the pool's reputation as a place of evil deeds. For, in 1679, Andrew Simpson worked as an ostler at the Red Lion in Leek. He was a headstrong young man looking for easy money, and so entered a life of crime as a highway robber. The Red Lion was an ideal place for him to choose his victims. For travellers, particularly farmers, often came to the inn for refreshments, and showed their money unwisely. One farmer stayed overnight at the establishment with the intention of going on to Nantwich in Cheshire the next day. Simpson offered to show him the right road, and accompanied him for the first few miles. When they came to a wood, Simpson murdered the traveller and threw his body into a disused coal pit.

His next victim was a woman who had come to Leek Market to sell cloth, lace and thread. He overheard her boasting of how well she had done and was determined to relieve the trader of her money on her way back to Bakewell. The woman's route took her past Blackmere and, at this isolated spot, Simpson jumped out on the cloth-seller and strangled her. Then he stole her purse and boxes of lace and linen. Simpson tied a rope around her middle and fastened a big stone to the other end. He then picked up the dead woman and tossed her into the pool.

The ostler made a mistake when he went into a nearby inn and gave some of the stolen goods to a maidservant. She became suspicious and, at the first opportunity, roused the authorities. The pool was dragged and the body was recovered from the water. Simpson was arrested and later hung for the murder of the Bakewell woman.

Another tale of violence connected with the Mermaid's Pool also took place in the 17th century. One stormy Autumn evening, a group of locals were sitting round the cheerful fire in The Cock Tavern, which stood on the corner of Leek Market Place, when in came a well-known town butcher. He remarked on the wild night and went on to say that it would be a brave man who would venture abroad, especially if he had to go across the moors near to the haunted mere. Surprisingly, a young man took up the challenge and wagered that, for a crown, he would walk there and back that night to the Blackmere. He proposed to go armed only with a stout cudgel, which he would leave at the pool as proof that he had been there.

The next morning, a few of his cronies would go across the heath to find the stick at the mere. The money was raised by the company and the bold fellow set off across the desolate moors.

The man walked briskly, determined to reach the pool as soon as possible. Eventually he came near to the Blackmere and heard the distressed cries of a woman. He stayed still and listened again. The screams were louder this time, but what could he do? He was alone and unarmed, except for his cudgel. Then a clever idea came to him, he started to shout for his imaginary friends to come to his aid. "Tom, Jack, Harry, this way, we'll get the rogue!" The woman heard him and called for help. The man

The Mermaid Inn.

approached as far as he dared and saw a female lying on the banks of the tarn. There was no sign of the attacker, his ruse must have worked and the man had fled from the spot. The wretched woman had been beaten up and almost stripped of her clothes. Her rescuer helped her to her feet and they made their way back to Leek. On the way, she explained that her lover had got pregnant and was not willing to saddle himself with a wife and child. He had enticed her to that isolated pool with the intention of drowning her in the deep water. When the weary travellers arrived back at the Cock Tavern they found some of the company still huddled around the fire. The young man was treated as a great hero after the tale had been related to his mates, and, with the woman to verify his every word, the wager was paid in full without any hesitation.

Half a mile south to the Blackmere Pool stands the Mermaid Inn, said to be the third highest licensed house in England. In the past it was an old drovers inn, known as Blackmere House, when herds of cattle were driven from Congleton through Leek, Hartington, Winster and on to Nottingham. Now it is a popular rendezvous for the motorists who drive over the windswept moors.

2. MURDER MOST FOUL

John Nadin was born at Hores Clough near Leek. Although his parents were poor, they encouraged their son in his schooling, as he showed an aptitude for learning.

They were immensely pleased when he obtained a job with a wealthy farmer called Robert Brough to manage his estate at White Lee, Danebridge.

John was a tall, slim, handsome young man and well liked in the Brough household. He was all set for a successful future career, and his status improved even further when he rescued Robert Brough from drowning in the flooded River Dane.

Julia Brough was much younger than her husband, and was very attracted to John Nadin. They started to meet in secret and Julia gave him a ring, saying that it was a token of her deep love for him, and if anything should happen to her husband she would be happy to marry him.

Rumours started to circulate amongst the household, as the maids gossiped and the farmhands began to talk about the affair. Eventually the scandal became known in Leek tongues wagged in the taverns, especially in the Cock Inn. Mr Stratham, the host, felt duty bound to warn his friend Robert Brough about "the goings on," that he had heard about from his customers.

Julia became more and more persistent as time went on, that John should murder her husband. Three or four years after she gave John the ring, Julia told her lover that the deed must be done without delay. If he refused to do it, she would perform the task herself. At last she wore down Nadin's doubts and he went to lie in wait for his master who had gone to Congleton market.

He found he could not carry out such a dastardly act, and came back to the farm. Julia was very angry with him when she found out that he had failed to kill her husband. In the meantime, Mr Brough came to the conclusion that there might be some truth in the stories he had heard about his wife and John, so he decided to dismiss Nadin.

Over the next few days Nadin was shocked by his employers decision to be rid of his services. He came to the same conclusion as Julia that Brough must be murdered, so a fortnight after the first attempt he tried again. Nadin followed the farmer to Leek and kept watch for him on his return that night. As Brough came along the lonely track across the moors, little did he realize he was walking that way for the last time. The old man was tired and trudging wearily towards home, when suddenly he was knocked to the ground by an assailant. Nadin then savagely slashed at his master's face, neck and wrists with a knife.

The ex-employee left the body on the roadway and hastened back to White Lea. Julia was waiting anxiously for him, but their satisfaction at getting rid of Brough was short lived, when John realized that he had left the murder weapon beside the body. At three o'clock in the morning Mrs Brough went out alone to the scene of the crime. When she came upon her husband's corpse, she found the knife and threw it over a hedge. Then she took money and items out of Brough's pockets, to make it look like a highway robbery and returned home. Julia then advised Nadin to put the blame for the crime on a neighbour, a William Wardle. He was a peddlar who had, had an argument with the dead man.

But Nadin made a bad mistake when he ventured into a tavern at Dane Bridge. The young barmaid who served him noticed his agitated manner and blood stains on his clothes. Soon afterwards he was arrested and appeared before the Coroner, Thomas Palmer. After being examined by Magistrate Thomas Hollinshead of Ashenhurst, he was transferred to Stafford gaol. At his trial John Nadin pleaded not guilty, and laid the blame on William Wardle, but witnesses brought forward on Wardle's behalf were able to clear his name and the peddlar was acquitted.

The evidence against Nadin was too strong, for he was found guilty and sentenced to hang on Tuesday the 3rd of August 1731. In fact Nadin confessed to murdering his master with his own knife, and that Brough's wife had been his mistress.

John Nadin was very penitent after the trial and gladly accepted visits from Rev. Corn whilst he was in prison. The Reverend gentleman accompanied him from Stafford to Leek on the night before he was hanged where he lodged under an armed guard at the Cock Inn in Leek.

Crowds of people gathered at White Lea to watch the execution of John Nadin. It was a very hot day when the macabre procession started off from Leek to the home of the late Robert Brough. Choristers from Leek, Bosley and Winkle sang psalms as they walked along.

The hangman was behind Nadin and held the rope around the condemned man's neck, like a halter. The chains and ladder were carried by other officers.

The gallows was an apple tree in the garden of the murdered man. From a stout branch hung the rope, and at twelve o'clock, mid-day John Nadin mounted the ladder. He asked William Wardle to forgive him, and the hangman slipped the noose around his neck. Nadin met his doom and his body hung there for three quarters of an hour. It was cut down and taken by cart to Gun Heath, where the corpse was left hanging in chains on a gibbet twenty-one-feet high.

3. AN UNTIMELY DEATH

The village of Rushton Spencer lies in a valley near to the Cheshire border, where its tiny church stands high on a ridge overlooking magnificent hilly countryside. The church is dedicated to St. Lawrence the martyr, and is a curious building of wood and stone. It dates back to the reign of King John, and was constructed of massive timbers taken from the surrounding forest. The church was known as the "Chapel in the Wilderness." When the original wooden building began to decay in the 17th century, the chapel was encased in stone. The little church is unique in the county, and has a weather-boarded bell tower, mullioned windows and a rare 13th–century timbered nave. In the churchyard, sheltered by tall firs and gloomy yews, lies the grave of Thomas Meaykin. The words on the crumbling headstone give a hint of the sinister tale of a young man, who was said by some to have been buried alive. The inscription on the tombstone states:

> *"Thomas Meaykin, son of Thomas and Mary Meaykin*
> *interred July 16th 1781, aged 21 years.*
> *As a man falleth before wicked men. So fell I."*

The unique church at Rushton Spencer, dedicated to St. Lawrence the Martyr.

Thomas Meaykin was born in Rushton Spencer and when he reached manhood he looked to the market town of Stone for an occupation. He obtained a position as a groom to the local apothecary. Thomas had a way with animals and enjoyed his work. He would often be seen around the small town exercising his master's string of horses. Meaykin had an amiable personality and soon made many friends in the locality. His handsome features attracted the attentions of the apothecary's daughter, who was a pretty girl, and used to getting her own way with her doting father. Whether or not Thomas returned her affections is unknown. The apothecary was appalled when he found out about his daughter's infatuation with one of his servants. He had more ambitious plans for her future than for her to become the wife of a mere groom.

Not long afterwards the young man was struck down by a mysterious illness. His condition deteriorated before his parents could be summoned to his bedside. He was hastily buried in the churchyard of St. Michael's at Stone. Many rumours circulated about the town concerning the youth's puzzling death. It was said by some that he had died of a contagious disease, others muttered darkly about poison being administered by the apothecary.

As the weeks and months passed by, Thomas Meaykin's tragic death was forgotten, until nearly a year later, when a strange incident took place in St. Michael's churchyard. The new groom of the apothecary was driving a pony past the church, when the animal escaped into the churchyard. The pony started to scrape the ground over Meaykin's grave, as though to tear up the earth. The small horse had been a particular favourite of the dead man, and due to the animal's peculiar behaviour, the suspicions of Meaykin's friends were once more aroused about the cause of his death. It was decided to exhume the body. A terrible truth was revealed when the coffin was opened. They found that Meaykin's corpse was lying face downwards, instead of face upwards, which clearly indicated that he had been buried alive. It was surmised that the young groom had been given a powerful narcotic, which gave the appearance of death. Before the effect of the drug had time to wear off, the body had been committed to the ground. His grieving relatives removed his remains to the place of his birth.

Meaykin's grave in the churchyard of Rushton Spencer is the only one to face west instead of east, the intention being to prevent his tormented spirit from wandering over the surrounding countryside.

Thomas Meaykin's gravestone, Rushton Spencer Church.

4. THE HEADLESS HORSEMAN

The moors of North Staffordshire cover some 300 square miles. They abound with weird and wonderful tales, which have been passed down through the generations. One such tale is of "*The Headless Horseman.*"

This unearthly creature haunts the moors on his white horse. In his former life he was a great warrior and leader. He led his followers into battle in Yorkshire between the Scots and the English. His men fought well, but the opposing side had a far larger army. Their leader urged them on and in a last desperate bid, he rode in to the middle of his foes, slashing his enemies down on every side with his mighty sword. At last the warrior was overcome and his head was struck from his body. One of the dead hands of the leader still clutched a jewel studded staff which he had held at the time of his decapitation. The faithful horse carried his master's body back to his home on the Staffordshire moorlands.

But his spirit did not rest for long, and for whatever reason it was doomed to roam cross the moors until the end of time. Over the centuries his ghost became known as the Headless Horseman. Old records give a very vivid description of his appearance. His body is encased in a kind of armour, which seems to glow as if it contained an inner fire. From his neck a cloak hangs down which is made of a golden material, and covers the haunches of the animal. In his right hand he carries a staff or baton. The position of the horse is peculiar, because its fore and hind legs extend as though it has been stopped instantaneously whilst in the act of galloping!

One version of the story tells of a farmer from Onecote, who was returning to his home on the lonely moor, after being to the market at Leek. He was in a rather befuddled state of mind after drinking too much ale at his favourite tavern in the town.

On the track in front of him he thought he recognized a neighbour on horseback. Thinking that he would get a lift home, he called after the man and before he knew what was happening, he found himself jerked violently onto the back of the animal. Too late, and to his horror he realized that the rider was none other than the Headless Horseman. He tried desperately to dismount but the horrible apparition on the horse in front of him would not release him. The horse sprang away clearing hedges, fields and ditches in a few bounds. Leaving the unfortunate traveller, at one moment feeling his legs brushing the tops of the trees and the next minute down hard over the heathland. At last the headless rider deposited the man outside his own back door, groaning and bruised from head to toe. The luckless fellow died a few days later from his awful battering.

Staffordshire Moorland, haunt of the "Headless Horseman".

Another tale tells of a more fortunate wayfarer, who was also crossing the moors, but this time on horseback, accompanied by his dog. As the farmer was jogging his way home from an errand on a dark, moonless night, he was anticipating with pleasure the warm meal that his wife would be preparing for him at that very moment. Suddenly he was joined on the road by the Headless Horseman, who lifted his staff and pointed it at the farmer. Now the farmer knew all the tales of this dreaded emblem of authority, so he turned his head away quickly and refused to look at the apparition. In doing so he saved his own life because it was said whoever the Headless Horseman pointed at with his staff would die soon afterwards. The farmer broke out in a profuse sweat, his horse trembled violently and the dog howled dismally. However the man managed to get home safely. The next day the poor horse dropped dead whilst out ploughing and the dog died a few days later. The farmer was shaken for a good while by his experience, and made sure that he never crossed the moors again at night.

The Headless Horseman has been seen in more modern times by the passengers of a coach, who were travelling in the area near to Longnor. The temperature in the bus became very cold after the sighting, luckily, no one seems to have had any ill effects after the incident.

Lud's Church

5. THE LEGEND OF LUD'S CHURCH

Lud's Church is one of the secret places of North Staffordshire. A deep, chasm set in spectacular countryside, near to the Cheshire border. An area of wild moors, craggy hills and many legends. Lud's Church lies in the Dane Valley at the top of a steep hill near to Castle Cliff Rocks. It is sometimes called Trafford's Leap by the locals, after one of squires of Swythamley Hall who leapt over the cleft on his horse whilst out hunting.

It is easy to miss this forbidding cleft, because the entrance is so narrow. Steps lead down into the chasm, where trees and undergrowth overhang to form a canopy or roof. This explains why it is sometimes called the Green Chapel. Water drips down the moss covered rocks, and the sun never shines in this eerie place. The twisting chasm is about one hundred yards long, forty feet deep and less than seven feet wide at the bottom. This gritstone gorge is a place of mystery and legend, said to be the work of the devil, a traditional hiding place of Robin Hood, and another old tale tells of the origin of its name.

Walter de Lud-auk became a zealous follower of Wycliffe who was called the "Dawning Star of the Reformation." His supporters were known as Lollards. Walter and his friends used to meet in this cleft in the summer months to practise their new religion in secrecy, safe from the prying eyes of the authorities, who suspected that they met in the area. Many searches were made for the Lollards but their meeting place was never found, owing to the dense forest that covered the hills. One of their chief protectors was Henrich Montair, the head forester, who would sometimes bring food and warn them of soldiers in the vicinity.

One fine summer afternoon the Lollards assembled in the gorge for a service. Their minister, Walter de Lud-auk stood on a rock and addressed them. He was 70 years of age, but upright in bearing. His hair was snow white, and his brow massive. He spoke with a melodious voice, and his fourteen companions listened to him with awe. For he was a fine teacher, intelligent with a strong will, and well able to bear the wrath of the Catholic Church.

Amongst the small congregation was Alice de Lud-auk, the beautiful eighteen year old granddaughter of their pastor. Her parents had died when she was only an infant and she had been left in the care of her grandfather. Alice often accompanied Walter on his journeys. She was a tall slim girl, who had been endowed with the family trait of dulcet voice. Near the entrance of the rocky crevice was Henrick Montair. He leaned against the cliff, a massive, powerful man, with dark hair and black beard.

He was dressed in Lincoln green cloth, with buckskins protecting his legs. He wore a belt, in which he carried a broadsword, a horn and a dagger. A crossbow and a sheaf of arrows lay at his feet.

The pastor led with a short prayer and then the opening hymn was sung. The Lollards sang a few verses and then Alice sang a solo, her voice rising sweet and clear on the still summers day. The singing was heard by the searchers who were hunting for the worshippers in the woods.

Before Montair could give any warning to the Lollards to escape through the far end of the cleft, the soldiers were at the entrance. Their leader waved his sword and cried, "yield in the name of the church and his Majesty King Henry the Fifth." The Lollards went to their weapons and were prepared to fight the intruders, but Lud-auk shook his head, so they desisted. Then the forester leapt forward and seized the officer in an iron grasp and threw him back into the midst of his followers. Montair drew his sword and shouted to the worshippers to escape through the other entrance, whilst he tried to hold the soldiers at bay.

One of the soldiers fired his arquebus at the forester but it just flew past his ear into the cleft. A loud shriek came from behind Montair, who turned and saw to his horror that Alice had been hit in the chest by the bullet. Henrich uttered a howl of despair, and threw himself upon his foes. The soldiers drew back from these terrible blows of the frenzied woodsman. Montair killed two men before pausing for breath. From within the chasm came the melancholy notes of a death chant, sung by the Lollards. Then Walter came out of the Green Chapel bearing the corpse of his grand daughter. His disciples followed him in solemn procession, some of them carrying pick-axes and spades. They stopped a few yards away from the entrance of their church, and dug a grave for Alice de Lud-auk. The soldiers did not prevent them and hung around in subdued groups. When the hole was deep enough the corpse lowered into the grave, and the earth carefully thrown on top.

Her grieving grandfather kneeled down, and called for his companions to do the same. Then the pastor offered up a short, fervent prayer. Walter rose to his feet and told the soldiers with dignity that he and his friends, including the forester would give themselves up to the authorities.

On their way to London, Montair conceived a plan of escape for the Lollards, but they refused to take part in the idea. However Walter realized that Henrich was likely to be sentenced to death for having killed two soldiers and interfering with the arrest of the Lollards. He instructed Montair to convey important documents to France for him. At first the forester refused to leave his friends to their fate, but on Walter's insistence

Lud's Church lies in the vicinity of Back Forest, north Staffordshire.

Montair made his escape and sailed for the continent, where he lived until the invasion of England.

Some of the Lollards were imprisoned for a short while and a few were pardoned. Walter's fate was never known, but it is presumed that he died in prison.

An oak tree grew over the grave of Alice de Lud-auk, and a wooden effigy once stood on a high ledge in the chasm. This was believed to be a likeness of Alice, but it was in fact a ship's figurehead. Whatever the truth of the tale about the secret worshippers, the cleft has been known as Lud's Church ever since.

6. FORGERS OF FLASH

The village of Flash is just off the A53 Leek to Buxton road, and is reputed to be the highest village in England. At 1,518 feet above sea level, it can also boast of having the highest public house, The New Inn, and the highest Post Office. It is a small place with only a handful of grey, stone houses, a sombre Victorian church and is the only centre of population in the parish. The huge Methodist chapel was built in 1821 and the school has closed, but the building is now used as the village Post Office.

Even today Flash is an isolated village, with magnificent views over the lonely moors. It was even more so in the last two centuries and an ideal spot for anyone with an inclination to dabble in unlawful pursuits. There are many myths and stories of counterfeiters who plied their dishonest trade from some of the more outlying cottages in the district.

One mile away to the north west of Flash lies Three Shires Head, on Axe Edge. This lovely dramatic place is where the counties of Cheshire, Derbyshire and Staffordshire meet. The River Dane winds through the enclosed valley, and where another stream converges with are two attractive stone bridges, rocky ledges, and several tracks by the wayside. The area can only be

One of the tracks which converge at Three Shire's Head.

The New Inn, Flash — the village is said to the the highest in England

reached on foot or on horseback, so it remains unspoilt, although it is very popular in the summertime as a picnic spot. In bygone days Panniers Pool, beneath the bridges would have been a welcome watering hole for the tired packhorses driven along the moorland tracks by their masters on the way to and from Buxton. It was an easy matter for the forgers to come to this lonely spot and elude the law officers by slipping into another county with their ill-gotten gains. It is believed that the slang term "Flash Money," meaning counterfeit coinage came from the village of Flash.

A sinister tale is said to have been connected with an inn further down the valley towards Danebridge. A pedlar from Flash called Ward-of-the-Brook, was travelling home one evening by way of Danebridge. Whilst in the vicinity of Lud's Church, a thick mist descended on the track. The pedlar decided to spend the night in a lonely wayside inn which he knew was close by. On entering the building, he found that he was the only customer on that dismal night. He paid for his drink and night's lodging and went over to sit by the fireside. Although Ward was relieved to have found shelter, the atmosphere of the place depressed him. He remembered some of the tales he had heard of the isolated hostelry, of travellers who stayed at the inn and were never seen again. There was a horrible rumour that the customers were killed for their money and parts of their bodies were made into pies. The landlord had certainly seemed a surly character and had little to say to the pedlar.

He was aroused from his reverie by a small girl who had come into the bar. "Are you staying for the night?" she asked. Ward smiled at her and said that he was. "I live here," she said, and took hold of one of his hands. "What fat hands you have, what nice pies they'll make." Then she ran out of the room.

The pedlar was filled with horror at the innocent remark of the child, and decided that he would be safer outside in the fog than stay in such an evil house. He made an excuse to the landlord that he thought he had dropped something outside, and left the tap room. To his surprise the mist had lifted and he could see his way quite well by the light of the bright moon.

Instinctively he took a little known foot path across the fields to Back Forest, instead of the normal route home to Flash. After he had gone a short way he thought he heard the baying of hounds. Swiftly he ran towards Blackbrook, and leaping from rock to rock across the stream he took refuge under Caisters Bridge, an arch within a few yards of the River Dane. He had no sooner hidden himself under the bridge, when he heard the dogs barking and men shouting in pursuit of him. The hounds traced his scent as far as the brook, but the water stopped them in their tracks. The pedlar who was only a few feet away from his pursuers waited until he thought it was safe to come out and then made his way back to Flash.

The next day Ward-of-the-Brook informed the nearest Justice of the Peace of what had taken place the night before. Parish constables were sent to the inn, which was searched and incriminating evidence found. The landlord and his accomplices were arrested on charges of murder and counterfeiting, taken into custody and duly punished for their evil crimes. For sometime the authorities had suspected that the inn was being used as the headquarters for a gang of coiners, who were also preying on unwary travellers, stealing their money and killing their victims.

The inn was demolished but it was rumoured that the ruins of the building were haunted, as strange noises were heard and flashing lights seen after darkness had fallen.

7. TALES OF THE ROACHES

The dramatic gritstone escarpment known as The Roaches lie in the Southern Pennines, a thousand feet above sea level. The Roaches stretch for three miles in length and two miles in breadth from east to west. The attractive market town of Leek is situated in a valley four miles to the east of this rocky outcrop.

In 1980 the Peak Park Planning Board purchased the Staffordshire Roaches, thus ensuring that walkers and climbers could enjoy exploring this marvellous swathe of countryside in peace. This acquisition ended 50 years of disputes and acrimony over public access to the area. Ramblers and climbers had been forbidden as far back as the 1930s, by the private owner of the land to walk or climb over the rocky escarpments and the surrounding moorland.

In 1977 the Swythamley estate was put up for sale, and the chance came for the Peak Board to buy the 1,000 acres which included The Roaches. However the scheme did not succeed for various reasons, even though the Board was eager to save this unique tract from being exploited or destroyed.

In the meantime the land had been bought by two farmers Mr Alan Edgecox and Mr Frank Sykes. They erected fences on the moorland with the idea of rearing 3,000 sheep. The plan was a failure and resulted in erosion and the loss of habitat necessary to deer, grouse and wallabies. The latter animals having escaped from a private zoo belonging to a member of the Brocklehurst family who lived at Roach House.

Many tales have sprung up about The Roaches, some of them mythical, some of them true. Many seem to centre around Rock Hall cottage, which is situated near to the round hill of Hen Cloud. It was built in 1850 as a lodge for the gamekeeper of Mr Brocklehurst, who owned the Swythamley estate. The building looks more like a mock folly than a house, with battlements, tower and pointed church-like windows. It is dwarfed by the massive peaks of rock which tower overhead, and has no running water or electricity. The last occupants were Doug Moller and his wife Anne, who lived there for twelve years until they left in 1989. Doug became a famous local character, known as *"The King and Lord of the Roaches."* He wrote a book entitled *"The Wars of the Roaches,"* describing their life at Rock Hall, and their struggle to survive in this harsh environment.

Before the gamekeeper's house was built there were said to be caves on the site, but the stone was removed to build cottages in the neighbourhood. One of these was known as "Rock Cave," and was occupied by a woman known as Bess Bowyer. She was born in the cavern in the 18th century,

Rock Hall

and lived there for nearly a hundred years. The cave was large and had a great number of fallen rocks inside, which Bess used to divide the dwelling into two rooms, one for day-time living and the other as sleeping quarters. There was a fresh spring of water flowing through the cave. Bess also took smugglers and deserters into her weird home, and helped them to escape the law by taking them through an opening at the back of the cavern which led out ono the rocky hillside. She was said to have been descended from a notorious mosstrooper who lived on the moors. He and his desperate wanderers used to impose blackmail on the hapless travellers through the surrounding countryside Bess had her reputed daughter living with her at one stage of her life. The girl was fond of singing and often on Summer nights, her fine, clear, voice could be heard over the hillside. To the local people who heard her the words seemed to be foreign and melancholy. One winter's morning Bess was seen to be in a state of great distress,and said that her daughter had been seized by strange men who took her away. Eventually old Bess was found dead in her lonely abode.

In 1860 a footpath was made along the ridge of The Roaches. On the track there is a small tarn called Doxy pool. It is dark and deep, and

Rockhall Cottage, almost invisible in the rocks and trees; it was originally built as a gamekeeper's home on the Swythamley Estate.

hundreds of feet above any other known spring in the district. Even in drought years it is said never to run dry.

Rock Hall cottage has had many visitors, but probably none as distinguished as when Royalty called at the house in the last century. A local journal gives a fascinating account of the visit.

"On August the 23rd in 1872 Prince Francis, the Duke of Teck and his wife Princess Mary Adelaide, the Duchess of Teck, passed through Leek to attend a picnic given by Mr Brocklehurst of Swythamley Hall. Rock Hall was the place selected amongst the wild crags and rocky precipices of the Roaches. The Royal couple were staying with the Earl and Countess of Shrewsbury for a few days at Alton Towers. The party travelled by train from Alton to Leek. Just after one o'clock in the afternoon the train steamed into the station. The procession passed through the town, where enthusiastic crowds numbering 9,000 were waiting to see the cavalcade. It made a colourful spectacle, the Summer sunshine with the outriders in their scarlet tunics. The equerries-in waiting, Captain Dausey and Mr Clements, and the bays and greys. The procession was headed by the Earl of Shrewsbury's brass band, followed by the Leek Rifles, and the fine band of the Corps. The cavalcade took the route up Canal Street, and St Edward Street, on through the Sheep Market and onto the Market Place, where the crowds were so dense that it had difficulty passing through. After an enjoyable drive through the romantic countryside they arrived at Rock Hall, where the Royal party were received by Philip Brocklehurst Esq. and Miss Brocklehurst. A pony carriage was waiting to take Princess Mary and Lady Shrewsbury as far as possible up the steep incline. The party then proceeded on foot to the 3rd summit of The Roach. They climbed up the winding flight of stone steps cut out of the solid rock to the top. Tents had been erected on the summit, and their interior decorated with the skins of wild animals. Facing the edge of the rock on the top. was the seat of honour for the princess. This was constructed of a huge hollow, hewn out of the rock. Cushions were placed in the hollow, and the surroundings covered with white satin and embroidered with the Royal Arms, and guarded round the face of the rock with a slender chain. Next to the seat flew the Royal Standard.

After luncheon the party descended to Rock Hall after spending three hours on the peak. The princess planted a Scotch fir tree nearby to commemorate her visit. the labourers on the estate had laid their coats on the green sward for a few yards. The Royal couple walked over the "path" to their carriage. The princess on being told that this was a voluntary act on the part of the workers, said she was touched by the demonstration of

The Roaches — a dramatic escarpment of gritstone rocks which lie four miles to the east of Leek.

good feeling and loyalty towards them, and went on to say how much she had enjoyed her visit among the wild scenery of The Roaches.

Rock Hall cottage became a listed building in 1987. The strange house has now become a climber's hut, as a memorial to the famous climber Don Whillans who died in 1985. A fitting choice as the rugged peaks above Rock Hall have been a favourite haunt for such enthusiasts for many years.

8. MUCKLESTONE AND ITS LEGENDS

Mucklestone lies in the lovely north-western corner of the county near to
Market Drayton. It is so peaceful here today, that it is difficult to imagine
that a desperate battle took place, one-and-a-half miles away to the south
west.

On the 23rd of September in 1459, the Battle of Blore Heath took
place between the Yorkists and the Lancastrians. It was won by the
Yorkists who had between 4,000 to 7,000 men, compared to the opposing
side who had a force of 10,000. Lord Audley who was in command of the
Lancastrians for the King, lived at Heighley Castle, close by. The Yorkist
force under the Earl of Salisbury carefully chose the best position on the
slope of the hill overlooking the small Hemphill brook. The Lancastrians
attacked, Salisbury made a show of resistance and pretended to retreat, but
when the opposition advanced towards the bottom of the valley, he

*This house in Mucklestone stands on the site of William Skelhorn's smithy. He is
reported to have reversed the horseshoes on Queen Margaret's horse in order to
confuse the pursuing Yorkist army when she made her escape after watching the
battle of Blore Heath from the top of St. Mary's Church tower.*

suddenly turned and fought back. Salisbury scored a complete victory, and Audley was killed in battle. The site where he fell is marked by a cross, which stands in a field on private land, opposite to Audley's Cross farm near Loggerheads, on the A53 road. There is an inscription on the stone pedestal which reads:

> *"On this spot was fought the battle of Blore heath in 1459. Lord Audley who commanded for the side of Lancaster, was defeated and slain. To perpetuate the memory of the action and the place, this ancient monument was repaired in 1765, at the charge of the Lord of the manor, Charles Boothby Skrymsher."*

William Skelhorn's anvil, St. Mary's churchyard, Mucklestone.

Queen Margaret, the fierce wife of the unstable Henry VI blamed the defeat on Lord Stanley, who had a considerable force of men at Newcastle-under-Lyme at the time of the battle. But Stanley made no effort to send them to Audley's aid. It is said that 2,400 Lancasterians died in the battle, but the fatalities for the Yorkists only numbered sixty.

Local tradition has it that on a small rounded hill, somewhere in the Fair Oak valley, that ten knights killed in the Battle of Blore Heath are buried in a row, with their faces turned towards a stream.

Legend has it in Mucklestone that Queen Margaret watched the battle from the top of the 14th-century tower of St Mary's church. After the defeat of her army Margaret rode to Eccleshall Castle, where she found hospitality and safety. Another legend which persists in this village is that the local blacksmith, William Skelhorn reversed the shoes on the horse to give the impression that the Queen was going in the other direction. A plaque on the house opposite to the church records this information.

> *"On this site stood the smithy of William Skelhorn at which Queen Margaret had her horse's shoes reversed to aid her escape from the Battle of Blore Heath, 23rd September 1459."*

Also in the churchyard facing the road, there is the anvil reputed to have come from the old village forge.

9. THE WITCH OF BURSLEM

The parish church of St. John the Baptist stands in a quiet corner of Burslem, on Cross Hill. The oldest part of the church being the short perpendicular west tower built in 1536.

Burslem is fondly known as the Mother Town of the Potteries, and was only a poor moorland village when the building of the church took place. In the churchyard lies the grave of Molly Leigh, the Burslem Witch.

The strange tale of Molly Leigh, this infamous character, took place in the 18th century. She was born in 1685 in a dark, half-timbered cottage on the edge of the moors. The house dated back to Elizabethan times, and stood at Hamil Grange, surrounded by woods, and was known as Jackfield. The cottage was divided into two sections. On the ground floor, one room served as a dairy with a well inside, and the other room was the living quarters with two bedrooms above.

Molly Leigh's grave, the churchyard of st. John the Baptist, Burslem.

27

Poor Molly had been born ugly, and as she grew older she became more and more eccentric. But even Molly had to earn her living and kept cows on pasture land, near to the Blue Stone Toll House. As the travellers passed by, they sometimes purchased milk from her and later told of the strange pet that Molly kept. It was a tame blackbird and perched on a hawthorn bush which neither blossomed nor bore fruit, near to her house. The blackbird could imitate all the birds in the woodland, and would often sit on her shoulder, as she went to Burslem to sell her milk from the dairy. Molly would shout at the top of her raucous voice, when she reached the community.

The villagers were frightened of her, for she had a vicious temper. She was often accused of watering down the milk, and stopping people's chimneys from drawing, but she earned enough money to keep herself from starving.

Unfortunately Molly fell out with the local parson. She didn't attend church, and the Rev. Spencer of St. John's church, declared publicly in the Turk's Head that Molly Leigh was a witch. The parson was a little too fond of imbibing and would spend much of his time in this hostelry. For a second time the clergyman made this statement in the inn. This time the information was passed on to Molly, who sent her pet to perch on the sign of the Turk's Head. The bird was said to have turned the beer sour and gave all the customers twinges of rheumatism. Parson Spencer said that the time had come to stop the nonsense and took his shotgun to Molly's lonely cottage, where he fired at the blackbird. His aim was poor and the blackbird flew away. For three weeks afterwards the parson suffered from severe pains in his stomach.

Molly Leigh died in 1746 aged sixty-one, and the folk of Burslem rejoiced. The Rev. Spencer, her one time enemy, had the task of conducting her funeral. It was a miserable wet day on the first of April, when they buried Molly in St. John's churchyard. The parson and the rest of the company retired to the Turk's Head, where they cheered themselves by drinking the strong ale.

Parson Spencer decided to carry on to Molly's cottage to make sure all was well. The would-be mourners followed and allowed him to take the first peep inside the dark dwelling. After a few minutes the terrified cleric ran out of the house, shouting that he had seen Molly sitting in her old chair by the fireside, mumbling and knitting. He said the words went something like this:

"Weight and measure sold I never,
milk and water sold I ever."

The parson and the mourners left the vicinity of the cottage as quickly as they could, stumbling back down the track to Burslem.

The Rev. Spencer sought the help of three other clergymen, from Stoke, Wolstanton and Newcastle to lay the spirit of Molly Leigh for ever. When the first stroke of midnight sounded over Burslem, the four clerics, led by Spencer, made their way into the churchyard. The men carried candle lanterns and the live blackbird, the pet of the departed Molly, which was said to have chirped "dismally." The grave was dug up and the coffin exposed, and the service of exorcism was held over the grave. It was then that the courage of Spencer's comrades deserted them and they fled leaving him to face his old adversary alone. Bravely the parson held the lantern high in one hand, and with the other forced open the coffin lid. Then he placed the light on a nearby tomb and took out the fluttering, protesting bird from its cage. He thrust it into the coffin and quickly closed the lid.

To make sure the Bogut (ghost) of Molly Leigh was laid to rest, her tomb was turned around north to south, opposite to all the rest of the graves.

For many generations the children would walk around her gravestone chanting, "Molly Leigh, follow me, Molly Leigh follow me." The table top tomb of Molly can still be seen on the south side of St. John the Baptist church, lying at right angles to the surrounding graves.

10. THE RESTLESS GHOST

The 17th-century Charnes Hall stands in a delightful park, just over a mile away from the village of Croxton. It was the home of the Yonge family for many centuries.

There is a gruesome tale connected with this handsome hall which is said to have happened nearly three hundred years ago. A Yonge wife in the prime of her life was suddenly taken ill. Her condition worsened and she sent for her family and retainers to come to her chamber and make their last farewells. The dying woman wore her favourite ring on her finger, and she made a last request that it should not be removed. One of the servants, a coachman, saw the ring with its glittering jewels on his mistress's finger and vowed he would steal the precious object.

That night as Mrs Yonge lay in her coffin in the family vault, the coachman crept into the chapel intending to carry out his evil deed. He had bribed the sexton to leave the vault door open. The servant prised the coffin lid up and gazed down at the dead woman. He lifted up the cold hand and examined the valuable ring which glinted faintly in the small pool of light cast from the candle he held in his free hand. The thief tried to force the ring off the finger but it would not budge, so he took out his sharp knife and hacked off the finger. To his horror blood spurted from the mutilated hand. The corpse groaned and sat up in her coffin. With a howl of fright the coachman grabbed the severed finger and fled from the burial chamber, never to be seen again. The shock of having her finger amputated awoke Mrs Yonge from her deep coma. Although weak and shaking she managed to climb out of the coffin. The poor woman staggered out of the chapel and across the park to the big house, the blood flowing from her maimed hand on to her white shroud.

Her husband sat alone in a downstairs room by the long window which opened straight out onto the lawn. Sorrowfully he thought of his beloved wife lying cold in her coffin. When there appeared before him at the window, an apparition of the dead woman. Shocked out of his reverie he jumped up, meaning to close the shutters to hide the awful sight. Then the figure put out her hand and tapped weakly on the window saying, "let me in husband for I am very cold."

The man saw red drops of blood on the shroud, and realized that his wife was alive. Joyfully he opened the window and helped Mrs Yonge into the room.

The lady recovered from her terrible ordeal and lived for many more years, before her final burial in the churchyard at Eccleshall. But not to rest in her grave, for her spirit came back to Charnes Hall, where her ghost is often seen gliding from room to room, searching for her missing ring.

The chapel at Charnes Hall is no more, but Chapel Wood lies opposite to the gateway of the mansion.

11. RED SOCKS OF BROUGHTON HALL

Broughton Hall is a beautiful black-and-white Elizabethan house situated off the B5026 between Loggerheads and Eccleshall. A long tree lined drive leads down to the mansion, with a belt of trees almost obscuring it from view, situated in the lovely, rolling, wooded quarter of north Staffordshire. The Broughton family lived at the Manor of Broughton from the 14th century, but it was Thomas Broughton who changed the modest, original dwelling into the large, four storied hall we see today. On the right lintel of the great, oaken, entrance door, are his initials T.B. and the date 1637 set below the window surmounting the door.

The Broughton family were catholic and Royal sympathizers in the Civil War, and Thomas Broughton along with other local gentry who supported Charles the First, were taken to Stafford by the Parliamentary soldiers, where they were imprisoned. Broughton estate was sequestered by the orders of the Staffordshire Parliamentary Committee and Broughton Hall requisitioned so that the soldiers were given free quarters at the mansion.

There is a tragic tale connected with this period of the history of Broughton Hall. The long gallery is a picturesque upper room, with a shining oak floor and great West Window. From this window one of the sons of the Broughton's is said to have leaned out and spied a troop of Roundheads turning into the drive. He shouted at them, "I am for the King." Suddenly a shot rang out, and the boy staggered back badly injured. The young Cavalier fell down bleeding profusely, but he managed to crawl from the gallery into one the adjoining rooms, where he died . His blood stained the floor, and could never be removed, until reconstruction work eventually obliterated the mark.

The ghost of the Broughton boy has been seen on many occasions since then, in the vicinity of the Long Gallery. He became known as "Red Socks", because of the scarlet stockings he wore at the time of his death.

There used to be a picture of a man in bygone costume in the last century called "Red Stockings", hanging on the wall between the dining room and the Great Hall. The portrait concealed the entrance to a secret hiding place, probably one that used to hide priests during the religous persecution of the Sixteenth Century.

One of the most intriguing accounts of a sighting of the *Broughton Ghost* is by a Miss Yonge in 1880, from nearby Charnes Hall. She was then a small girl of eleven and had hidden behind the door in the Long Gallery, when on a visit to the house and taking part in a game of hide and seek. The girl heard footsteps coming down the staircase which led to the attic.

Broughton Hall. The ghost of a boy, who was shot by rounndheads during the Civil War, is said to haunt the building wearing red stockings.

Thinking it was one of her friends coming to find her, she waited expectantly. But no-one came. Eventually the child ventured out into the Long Gallery and saw a young man looking out of the end window. He was wearing red stockings. Assuming it was one of the sons of the Broughton family who always wore knickerbockers and thick stockings, she crept past him, as he had his back to her. Thinking it was a good chance to get by without being seen, Miss Yonge rushed down the stairs to find everybody sitting down to tea. To her astonishment the young man of the house, that she had presumed was upstairs looking through the window, was already at the table. She went up to him and slapped him on the knee, saying,"how did you manage to get down before me, when I have just seen you in the Long Gallery and you didn't pass me on the stairs?" The youth looked puzzled and replied, "you couldn't have seen me because I haven't been in that room today."

The young girl had quite an argument with him, and his mother Lady Broughton, settled the matter by leading her small guest to the other end of the table, where she soon forgot about the strange event.

After the Civil War, Thomas Broughton was able to purchase his home again for the sum of three thousand pounds. Not that he had much time to enjoy his splendid house, for he died in 1648 and his son Brian inherited Broughton Hall. He had attended Charles the Second during his exile on the continent. Whilst being abroad Brian collected many art treasures and after the King's restoration to the Throne, brought these items back to Broughton. Charles conferred a Baronetcy on him in 1661, in recognition of his loyalty to the Crown.

The picturesque hall remained in the hands of the Broughton family until 1914, when it was bought by Mr John Hall, a Stafford industrialist, from Sir Delves Broughton. The mansion had been unoccupied for many years, as their principal home had been at Doddington, in Cheshire, from the 18th century. Broughton Hall was in great need of restoration and Mr Hall decided to take on this tremendous task. Owing to the advent of the First World War, the renovations were unable to begin until 1926. Then sadly Mr Hall died suddenly in 1930 before the work was completed. Mrs Hall carried on her late husband's ambition, for the benefit of their son John. A new wing was added to the house, copying the original syle.

Then tragically on the 9th of June 1934, John Hall aged twenty-two and heir to Broughton Hall, was killed in an accident in London.

From 1940 the house was used as a boy's preparatory school, until in 1951 Mrs J.Hall returned to make her home at the hall for a short period. In 1952 this lady donated the house to the Franciscan Missionaries of St. Joseph's, to be used as a Mother House of the Congregation. Broughton Hall is now privately owned.

12. THE SIEGE OF LICHFIELD CLOSE

The charming city of Lichfield is very historic, and renowned for its cathedral, one of the most graceful in the country and built of dark red sandstone. It has three slender spires which are unique and affectionately known as the Ladies of the Vale. The present cathedral was built in the 13th and 14th centuries and dedicated to St. Mary and St. Chad. The magnificent west front is decorated with 113 statues of saints, kings and bishops within its arcades and panels.

At the time of the Civil War, the citizens of Lichfield sided with the Parliament, but the authorities of the cathedral remained loyal to the King. In October 1642 a public meeting was held in the Guildhall. The Royalists were outvoted and a group of them went along to a house in Sadler Street belonging to Sir Richard Dyott, where they discussed the matter and agreed to raise a company of troops.

Lichfield was important to the Royalist armies as the main road to their headquarters at Oxford lay through the city. The south-coast ports were mostly garrisoned by the Parliamentarians, so it was vital for the King to get his supplies of imported arms and equipment from the north coast ports (which were mostly loyal to the crown) through the Midlands and on to Oxford.

The Cathedral Close was largely surrounded by water and fortified by walls. It was an ideal place for the Royalists to use as their garrison, which they held in February 1643, under the command of the Earl of Chesterfield.

Meanwhile the Parliamentarians marched into the county under the command of Lord Brooke, a fanatical puritan and an unswerving supporter of Parliament. Robert Greville, second Baron Brooke was born in 1608, the only son of Fulke and Mary Greville. When he was four years old he was adopted by his cousin, the first Lord Brooke. Soon after he was twenty-one he married Lady Catharine Russell, eldest daughter of the Earl of Bedford, by whom he had five sons. Lord Brooke was appointed by Parliament on 7th January as its Commander-in-Chief for the counties of Warwickshire, Staffordshire, Leicestershire and Derbyshire. He took Stratford-on-Avon by assault in February and soon secured Warwickshire for Parliament. The zealous General then advanced on to Lichfield with his army, his main aim being to destroy the cathedral. When he was a mile off the city he drew up his troops and prayed earnestly for a blessing on his intended actions. The Commander was able to march into Lichfield unopposed. He then placed his great guns against the south-east gate of the Close. There followed a dramatic event which took place on the first day of the siege, 2nd March 1643, which was described in this vivid contemporary account:

> *"While the gunners were attacking the gate in Dam street, Lord Brooke, who on that occasion resided in the house of Michael Biddle in the Market Place, was desirous of reviewing the attack in person. He was dressed in a plush cassock with a steel head piece which had five bars of gilt steel in front. He crossed the street to the house of one Richard Newbole, and through the entry of which he passed into the garden making his way in security behind the houses on the east side of the street; that he might reach the place where his piece was mounted. He entered the house of one Walter Franceyes, in Dam Street, in which had a very long passage, and was just opposite to where his piece was stationed, when lifting up his beaver that he might more clearly see what execution was done. He was observed by a gentleman, posted between the battlements of the high tower, known by the name of "Dumb Dyott", who shot him in the head and killed him. The Cavaliers attributed the direction of the fatal bullet to the influence of St. Chad; upon whose anniversary this memorable event happened, in resentment of the sacrileges this nobleman was committing upon the cathedral."*

There is a strong tradition that the man who shot Lord Brooke from the tower with his musket was the deaf and dumb son of Sir Richard. The Dyott family had played an important part in the history of Lichfield for centuries. It is said that Charles I bestowed a strange favour upon Dumb Dyott in recognition of his having shot Lord Brooke, that at his death he would be carried from Freeford manor, the family home at midnight by a torchlight procession. Then his body would be laid to rest in the Dyott Chapel in St. Mary's Church at Lichfield a mile away. All the descendants of Dumb Dyott were buried in this fashion until the end of the 19th century.

However, the rejoicing of the besieged Royalists at the death of their enemy did not last for long. On the 2nd March Sir John Gell arrived with reinforcements from Derby. The ruthless new Commander dealt harshly with some of the wives and relatives of those confined in the Close. He placed the victims in the firing line, so that they would be shot by their own kinsfolk. Even this cruel ploy did not make the Royalists surrender their garrison, and Sir John, frustrated at the lack of progress against the stubborn Cavaliers, obtained a large mortar piece from Coventry. This

Lichfield Cathedral.

engine was sited in Sir Richard's garden in Sadler street. The gunner was ordered to fire on the "Popish Cavaliers" with the formidable grenadoes. These large iron balls were filled with gunpowder and caused great damage to the fabric of the cathedral. It also demoralized the beleaguered opposition and terrified their women folk. The Earl, realizing that his stock of food and stores were getting low, reluctantly surrendered the Close to the Parliamentarians.

During the occupation of the cathedral by the Roundheads the building was vandalized in many ways. The monuments were broken up, the stained glass windows smashed, and valuable records of the church were burnt. The Commonwealth soldiers had little regard for the sanctity of the building for they stabled their horses in the main body of the church, and each day hunted a cat with hounds throughout the cathedral delighting in the echo from the vaulted roof.

The Parliamentarians did not hold the Close for long, as on the 8th April, Prince Rupert came to the rescue. He brought in miners from south Staffordshire to make a tunnel under the moat, which they drained. Explosives were then packed into the tunnel, and a section of the north wall was blown up. The Cavaliers were able to make a successful assault on the garrison, but the Roundheads defended it so well that their attackers had to retreat. However the Parliamentarians were now in such a weak position that they negotiated terms for an honourable surrender.

The third siege of Lichfield Close came in March 1646, and lasted intermittently until the July of that year. The attack upon the cathedral during this period was made by Sir William Brereton. He ordered his men to fire mortars at the highest steeple of the sacred edifice. After several days of bombardment the great central spire came crashing down, destroying the chancel, choir, organs and pulpit. The Parliamentarians regained their hold over the Close and held it for the next fourteen years. They left the cathedral in a ruinous state, and it remained so until after the Restoration of the Monarchy in 1660. Two years later Bishop Walter Hacket was appointed to the see. A popular tradition has it that on the first morning of his arrival, he awoke his servants at day break and sent them to set about clearing the rubbish from the cathedral with his own coach horses. Bishop Hacket worked tirelessly on his great task of restoring the "Mother Church of the Midlands". He generously contributed from his own resources to the rebuilding, which took eight years. The cathedral was reconsecrated in 1670.

13. THE LEGEND OF ST.MODWEN

For many centuries the town of Burton-upon-Trent has been associated with Saint Modwen. The parish church of Burton is dedicated to her. Modwen was the daughter of Mochta, an Irish Prince of the Clan Conalls, who ruled over a large territory from Iveagh to Armagh. In 630AD she founded a convent at Faugha in the county of Lough. It was around this time that Aldfrith, an English Prince, was staying in Ireland. He was the illegitimate son of King Oswin of Northumbria and had fled his country when his brother had succeeded to the throne. Aldfrith remained in Ireland and studied for a time. Eventually he decided to return to his own land and the Irish King Finnachta was intent on giving his English visitor a fitting present. Finnachta's coffers were empty so he sent one of his relations to rob a convent or church. The nobleman pillaged the convent of Modwen and gave the spoils to Aldfrith. The Abbess was, naturally, outraged by the theft of her property and followed the Prince to England. Modwen went to Whitby and sought an audience with the King, in 685AD, in the hope that he would rectify the wrong that had been committed. Aldfrith had now become King of Northumbria and promised to repay Modwen and invited her to stay at the double Monastery of Whitby, where his sister Elfleda was already living.

The Abbess resided in England for three years before making a pilgrimage to Rome. On her return journey she reached Burton-upon-Trent. Perhaps something about the terrain attracted her, such as the isolation of the small island in the River Trent, which made Modwen decide to stay. The Abbess built an oratory on the island in honour of Saint Andrew. The island became known as Andresia, St. Andrew's Isle, now known as Andresey Island. Modwen lived in the oratory for seven years as an anchoress. Whilst at Burton the Abbess gained a reputation for performing wonderful cures on people, by the application of water from a chalybeate well on Andresia. It became known as St. Modwen's Well and the local people used to decorate the place on the anniversary of her death.

Whilst at Andresia, Modwen received news of her brother Ronan who was an Abbot. He was working as a missionary in Scotland. Modwen went to join him in that part of the country where she founded many religious houses. The Abbess died at Lanfortin near to Dundee. A legend is told of her death. On the morning of her last day on earth, just as the grey dawn was breaking, two lay sisters went to her cell. As they approached they saw two silver swans (emblems of chastity) rise in the air. They were carrying the pure soul of the saintly Modwen to the borders of the "sea of glass unto crystal." The swans, which glide on the stretch of the river between the Island of Andresey and the site of the Abbey of Burton, have always been known as the Birds of St. Modwen.

In 874AD the Church of Andresia was wiped out by the Danes who came up the river. Although the buildings had been destroyed the Tomb of St. Modwen had been spared and a small community remained behind to care for the shrine. Perhaps the existence of this religious house persuaded Wulfric Spott, a rich nobleman of Mercia, to build his Benedictine Abbey at Burton which was dedicated to The Virgin and St. Modwen. The monastery was built on the west of the Trent, and the relics of St. Modwen were transferred from her tomb to a new shrine in the Abbey Church, which had a chapel dedicated to her.

The Benedictine Abbey built on the banks of the River Trent flourished and the town of Burton,which grew up around it, became a seat of learning. The abbey lasted until the Dissolution in 1540, under the reign of Henry the Eighth. During this time of oppression of the monasteries, all the shrines were dismantled and the bones of the Saints buried on the site. The old Abbey church became the Parish Church for the next two centuries. By 1700 the structure of the ancient building had become very dilapidated. It was said to be in a ruinous state and in danger of falling down. After much discussion and deliberations by the various bodies connected with the church it was decided to demolish it and build a new one.

The new Parish Church was built on the site of the old Abbey church, 1719–26, in the Palladian Style of dark sandstone. In the Church of St. Modwen there is a reminder of the legend of the Saint and the swans, which is beautifully depicted on the front of the altar.

St. Modwen is further remembered by this epitaph, which was said to have been inscribed on her shrine in the Abbey Church:

> *"Ireland gave Modwen birth;*
> *England a grave;*
> *Scotland her end; God he salvation gave;*
> *Life gives the first, her death the third earth gives*
> *The second earth her earthly part receives,*
> *Lanfortin takes whom Chief Tyr Connel owns,*
> *and favoured Burton keeps the virgin's bones."*

14. THE FASTING WOMAN OF TUTBURY

The small attractive town of Tutbury, with its ruined castle and ancient priory, is steeped in history and tradition. It is also where Ann Moore the notorious impostor lived in the last century. She claimed to have lived without food or nourishment from 1807 to 1813.

Ann Moore was born on the 31st of October, 1761, at Rosliston in Derbyshire, the daughter of a labourer named Pegg. She was a good looking girl, intelligent, but of a cunning disposition. In 1788, at the age of 27, she cajoled James Moore, a farm labourer, into marrying her. He deserted her soon afterwards but this didn't prevent her from becoming the mother of a large family. Around the turn of the century Mrs Moore made her way to Tutbury where she tried very hard to gain employment by honest means. Being unsuccessful she was reduced to dire poverty, setting off a chain of events which led her to make incredible claims. Because she was so poor, Ann found it necessary to exist on very little sustenance. Her long fasts created great interest amongst her neighbours which probably encouraged her to deceive the general public. Ann told everybody that she had lost all interest in food since 1806. This aroused local curiosity in her even more and, after six months, she took to her bed permanently. On the 20th of May, 1807 she said that after attempting to eat a biscuit, she had felt great pain and afterwards vomited blood. The last food she ever took was a few currants on the 17th of July of the same year and a month later she also reduced her liquid intake.

Fantastic theories were put forward by learned writers in various pamphlets of the time about the phenomenon of Ann Moore who could live without food. One writer claimed that Ann Moore lived on air, another that she had a diseased oesophagus which enabled her to live for long periods without nourishment. A third writer was convinced that Mrs Moore's fasting was made possible by divine intervention.

It was not long before Ann's incredible assertions attracted the intention of two local doctors, Robert Taylor and John Allen. They both communicated to the Medical Journal in 1808 about the strange case of Ann Moore. In September of that year an investigation committee was set up consisting of important members of the community. They took it in turns to watch Mrs Moore for four successive hours, which lasted for 16 days and nights. Bulletins were given out from time to time on Ann's progress. At the end of the vigil the committee came to the conclusion that the woman had been telling the truth when she claimed that she could exist without food. It was later supposed that she had been able to

Dog and Partridge, Tutbury.

deceive the watchers with the help of her daughter Mary Moore who visited her night and morning and passed food to her whilst in the act of kissing her mother.

Over the next four years, hundreds of sightseers flocked to the house in Ludgate Street to gaze at Ann Moore, "The Fasting Woman of Tutbury." They usually found her siting up in bed supported by pillows, with a large bible in front of her and uttering insincere opinions about religion and morals. Her curious visitors seldom left without leaving a sum of money.

Then, in the August of 1812, Doctor Alexander Henderson, a well known medical man, and his companion Mr Lawrence, assistant surgeon of St. Bartholomew's hospital, stopped at Tutbury. They were going on holiday to the Lake District but broke their journey in Staffordshire intending to visit Ann Moore. They found her at home and asked her some very detailed questions. She answered in a strong, clear voice, and told them that she had lost all desire for food and water. The only moisture that passed her lips was when she washed her face, once a week. She could not open her mouth properly because of the severe pain behind her jaws. Ann said that she had not slept properly for three years and was subject to fits.

Doctor Henderson and Mr Lawrence, however, were suspicious of Ann's statements for she looked too healthy for a woman of over fifty who claimed to have starved herself for so long. Her pulse was strong, her eyes, skin and mouth were moist like those of a normal person. She seemed to be of a reasonably sane mind, according to Doctor Henderson, who had made some inquiries into Ann's background. He found out that she had once posed as a woman of deep religious beliefs, until she had been exposed as an impostor. It was quite obvious to the doctor that she was a character who enjoyed the sensation she was causing in the small town.

Much to Ann's disgust, it was decided to carry out a further investigation into her unrealistic claims. A new committee was formed consisting of Dr. Garlic, Sir Oswald Moseley and the Reverend L. Richmond. A new bed was bought and weighed, and no one was allowed into her bedroom except the investigators. The strict vigil was started on the 21st of April 1813, and went on for nine days. By this time it was obvious that the woman was very sick indeed. She had become so weak that she wasn't expected to survive the ordeal. Ann was allowed a sip of vinegar and persuaded to sign a confession in which she admitted she was a fraud. Ann said that, during the time of her so called fast, she drank tea and ate apples. The investigators were lenient with her now that they had achieved their

The ruins of Tutbury Castle.

objective. They were amazed at how quickly she recuperated and all agreed that she could exist on very little sustenance.

Her deception aroused the wrath of the local people and Ann and her daughter were driven out of town. The residents of Tutbury heard no more of the two women until a few years later when mother and daughter appeared in Macclesfield and Knutsford courts on various charges, including stealing items from their lodgings. Nothing more was heard of them again and it is not known when or where Ann Moore died.

15. THE DEMON DONKEY

The Potteries have always produced unusual characters, with their own particular brand of eccentric behaviour. Hanley had one such individual in the 1790s, who was known as Sauntering Ned. He lived in a small straw, thatched hovel in Saggar Row. It now has the more refined name of Parliament Row. Although he was a half soaked fellow, he had to earn his living like everyone else down his street. but he would often take days off work and wander about the countryside, watching the wildlife. This was all very well, but the patience of his employer Mr Toft, finally wore thin and he had to sack him. He was sympathetic with his unreliable employee and probably realized that Ned wasn't as simple as he made out.

Mr Toft suggested to Ned that it might be a good idea if he became a hawker and sold pots to the surrounding villages. So in 1797 Ned took to the roads around Hanley, selling pottery from a large basket. He did so well that he had to buy a donkey to carry the on panniers strapped to the animal.

The roads in the country at that time were narrow with deep ruts, a morass of mud in the winter and dusty tracks in the summer. His journeys often took him to markets of Leek and Cheadle, and he would often make his long way back home in the dark. Ned decided he needed some protection from possible foot-pads. He came up with a bizarre idea, of rigging his donkey up as a demon. Ned made a devil's face mask complete with horns which he fixed over his donkey's head, before he approached certain lonely stretches of road which gave good cover for robbers.

A flickering candle was tied between the two horns, and for good measure a chain was fastened to the animal's legs, which rattled and clanked in a most uncanny way, which must have sounded like a supernatural spirit abroad in the dark night and hopefully would have frightened off most would-be attackers.

One dark, and wet, windy night, Ned was making his way back to Hanley from Cheadle, where he had, a good day selling his pots. As the hawker approached Bucknall Church he decided to put the mask over his donkey's head. It was nearly midnight and the churchyard at Bucknall was a very dark and dismal place, with its tall, swaying, trees.

To his surprise he saw that there was a horse and cart tethered by the gate. Ned led his little donkey through the open gate and into the cemetery. He stopped for a moment, hoping to see any sign of the owner of the horse and cart. But it was a black night, and the light from the candle on the animals head gave very poor visibility. Then he thought he heard the muffled sounds of digging coming from a grave nearby.

"What on earth is going on," thought Ned. He led the donkey to the edge of the open grave. The chain on the animal clanked and chinked as it moved forward. From the depths of the hole the digging stopped as the two men were just about to open the coffin that they had revealed. They looked up and saw to their horror a horned apparition staring down at them.

"Jim, it's the devil himself come for us," cried one of the men, and scrambling and slipping on the wet earth they both clambered out of the grave as fast as they could. Without a backward glance the grave robbers fled from the cemetery and were never seen again.

Ned had the best laugh he had, had for years. He pondered on what to do with the abandoned horse and cart. The hawker decided that he couldn't leave them there for the night. Firstly he took off the donkey's disguise, and then he hitched the animal behind the horse and cart and made his way home.

It was not surprising that the two resurrectionists never claimed their property. Ned kept the horse and cart and was able to expand his business. He saved enough over the next few years to buy a small pot bank and change from selling pots to making them.

One small mystery was never solved by the neighbours in Eaves Lane, near to Buchnall church. A thatched cottage had stood empty in the lane, where a family had recently died of an infectious disease. Two strangers had moved into the house which caused raised eyebrows. They seemed well-off, but did not appear to have any occupation. Also they owned a good, strong horse and a well made cart, but did not seem to put it to any good use. Then to the surprise of their neighbours, the men disappeared over night. There was much speculation as to what might have happened to them, but no one could ever have guessed the real reason.

ACKNOWLEDGEMENTS

Mr. and Mrs. J. Bradbury of Penkhull.
Pat Drozdecki and Eileen Hill of Burton-upon-Trent.
Mr. Harold Bode of Leek.
Pat and Brian Simpson of Grindon.
The staff of the following libraries: City Library, Hanley;
Leek Library; Nicholson Institute; Lichfield Library; and
Burton-upon-Trent Library.

THE AUTHOR

Marian Pipe was born in Hanley, Stoke-on-Trent, and grew
up in the area. She now lives in Kettering, Northamptonshire,
with her husband Dave. Marian has written several county
books on the supernatural and folklore, including
Northamptonshire and Leicestershire.

S.B. Publications publish a wide range of
local history titles. For a complete list of titles
available, please write (enclosing S.A.E.) to:–

S.B. Publications,
c/o 19 Grove Road,
Seaford,
East Sussex BN25 1TP